Cursive Writing

With a Twist!

by Kama Einhorn

S C H O L A S T I C
PROFESSIONAL **B**OOKS

New York • Toronto • London • Auckland • Sydney • Mexico City • New Delhi • Hong Kong • Buenos Aires

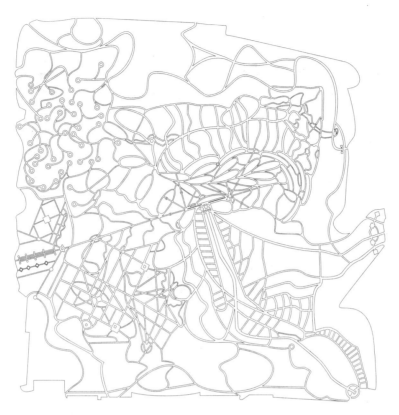

For Lucas Monaco

Cover design by Maria Lilja

Cover illustration by Michael Moran

Copyright page art by Lucas Monaco

Interior design by Ellen Matlach Hassell
for Boultinghouse & Boultinghouse, Inc.

Interior Illustrations by Michael Moran and Manuel Rivera

ISBN 0-439-31663-4

Printed in the U.S.A.

9 10   40   09

Aa Bb Cc Dd Ee Ff Gg Hh Ii Jj Kk Ll Mm Nn Oo Pp Qq Rr Ss Tt Uu Vv Ww Xx Yy Zz

Contents

Introduction

Welcome!

Practice makes perfect—and that's especially true for children who are learning to write cursive. Mastering this skill is often seen by children as a rite of passage—it's the kind of writing grown-ups do. As adults, it's easy to forget that our writing system asks children to learn four different forms of each of the 26 letters (upper- and lowercase print, upper- and lowercase cursive)! When children can automatically write each letter without having to labor over it too much, their minds are freed up for higher-level thinking. Children will read with more fluency. They'll also write faster, their mental energy devoted to expressing their thoughts on paper rather than to forming each individual letter correctly.

Making Handwriting Practice Fun

These fun, reproducible writing practice pages have many benefits:

Just like any skill, cursive handwriting requires practice and lots of fine-tuning before letter formation and recognition become automatic. These sheets provide that practice.

You can individualize instruction, handing out worksheets that will help each child with particular skills or letter formation.

The more that children are engaged in playful writing activities, the more likely they are to associate writing with pleasure—and do more of it!

Using This Book

Each reproducible page in this book can be used for whole-group instruction or individual practice. You might keep reproducibles at the writing center and allow children to choose from among them freely, or send them home as homework.

In Section 1, **Better Letter Practice Pages**, you'll find reproducibles that reinforce individual letter formation practice. Letters are grouped by similarity of formation. For instance, the cursive letters *a, d, g, q, o,* and *c* all begin with a backward, downward stroke ("Downhill Daredevils"!). The "better letter tips" on each practice page help children fine-tune and self-assess their writing.

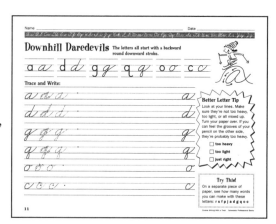

4

In Section 2, **Writing Practice Pages**, you'll find engaging reproducibles that get children writing. Each page emphasizes a different letter's formation. Tongue twisters, silly alliterative writing prompts, and more present invitations to write that kids can't resist!

Tongue twisters, in particular, provide auditory learners with additional reinforcement of letter sounds. You might also point out that in tongue twisters, the sounds seem to run together, and in cursive, the letters run together (are connected)!

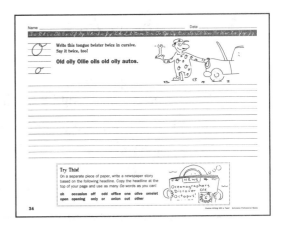

Section 3, **Games and Puzzles**, offers children fun, relaxing opportunities to read and write cursive and play with each letter in different contexts. Word searches, anagrams, scramblers, pangrams, acrostics, and other activities give children plenty of playful writing practice—and make them *want* to write!

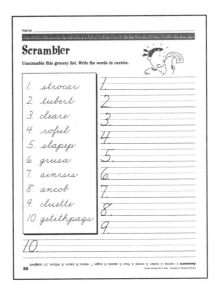

In addition, reproducible stationery (pages 60–61) gives children a chance to show off their new skills. You'll also find a make-your-own mini-book (page 62) and a "tent strip" (page 63) that your students can assemble and use for reference.

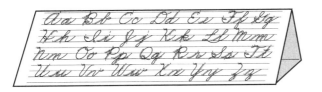

5

Other Ways to Make Handwriting Practice Fun

- Let children **practice writing with a variety of utensils**, not just pencils: colored pencils, metallic and glow-in-the-dark markers, fluorescent highlighters, glitter pens—anything that writes!

- Have children **practice writing on various surfaces**: They can use chalk on the sidewalk, trace letters into a flat "clay tablet," paint large letters onto sheets of newspaper, and use their fingers to form letters in a thin layer of shaving cream, sand, pudding, or finger-paint.

- **Incorporate all modalities**: For kinesthetic learners, have children form letter shapes with their bodies or trace letters onto one another's backs. For auditory learners, "talk through" each letter's formation. For tactile learners, involve the sense of touch (see above).

- Ask children to help you **make signs and labels in cursive** to display around the room.

- **Eat some letters**! Cook spaghetti and use it in class to form letters and words. You can also try cheese or honey (the kinds that come in squeeze-top containers) or licorice.

- Use the chalkboard. Let children **practice their letters on the board** so that they can see them at eye level. You might make permanent guiding lines with masking tape. In addition, you can wet sponges and "write" with them—a great way to clean the board! Children can watch their letters disappear as the water dries.

- Take it outside. **Use sidewalk chalk** on the playground surface, form letters with jump ropes, or have the children form giant letters with their bodies.

Better Letter and Writing Practice Pages

Name _____ Date _____

Mountain Climbers The first stroke in all these letters goes uphill.

i t u w e l

Trace and Write:

Better Letter Tip

Make your small letters small
and your tall letters tall.

Cursive Writing With a Twist! Scholastic Professional Books

Try This!

On a separate piece of paper,
practice writing *it, we, wet,* and *tie.*

Name _____

Date _____

More Mountain Climbers

l   l

b   b

h   h

k   k

Trace and Write:

Better Letter Tip

Check to see that all your letters are "behaving"! Are they sitting nicely on the lines? Are they all slanted in the same direction?

My letters are ☐ behaving ☐ misbehaving

Try This!

On a separate piece of paper, see how many words you can make with these letters: **i t u w e u l b h k**

Cursive Writing With a Twist! Scholastic Professional Books

9

More Mountain Climbers

r   s   f   p   j

Trace and Write:

Better Letter Tip

Are your letters closed up where they should be?

☐ yes   ☐ no

Try This!

On a separate piece of paper, draw your ultimate pair of pj's (pajamas!) and decorate them with *p*s and *j*s.

Downhill Daredevils

The letters all start with a backward round downward stroke.

a a a   d d   g g g   q q q   o o o   c c c

Trace and Write:

a a a

d d d

g g g

q q q

o o o

c c c

Better Letter Tip

Are your lines too heavy, too light, or all mixed up? Turn your paper over. If you can feel the grooves of your pencil on the other side, your lines are probably too heavy.

☐ too heavy

☐ too light

☐ just right

Try This!

On a separate piece of paper, see how many words you can make with these letters: **r s f p j a d g o c**

Cursive Writing With a Twist! Scholastic Professional Books

Aa Bb Cc Dd Ee Ff Gg Hh Ii Jj Kk Ll Mm Nn Oo Pp Qq Rr Ss Tt Uu Vv Ww Xx Yy Zz

Lumpy Letters

These letters all have lumps and bumps!
They go uphill and curve over.

n n m m v v x x y y z z

Trace and Write:

Better Letter Tip

Remember that *n* has two lumps and *m* has three.

Try This!

Look back at all your cursive letter practice and notice your style of handwriting. Do your letters usually slant forward, backward, or point straight up?

☐ **forward**

☐ **backward**

☐ **straight up**

Cursive Writing With a Twist! Scholastic Professional Books

Name _____

Date _____

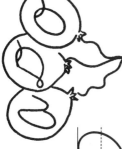
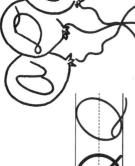

Backward Balloons

These capital letters look like big, round balloons. The first stroke moves backward.

A a   O O   D d   C C   E e   Q Q

Trace and Write:

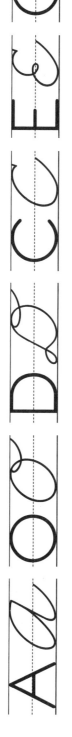

Better Letter Tip

When you write in cursive, remember the three Ps: pencil, posture, and paper. Hold your pencil properly, keep your feet on the floor, and slant your paper with the left bottom corner pointing toward your belly button. Lefties should point the right bottom corner toward their belly buttons.

Try This!

On a separate piece of paper, draw a bunch of balloons, each one formed by a different cursive letter from this page. Color them!

Cursive Writing With a Twist! Scholastic Professional Books

Name _____ Date _____

Lefties

The first stroke of these letters moves backward, to the left.

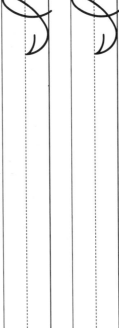

Trace and Write:

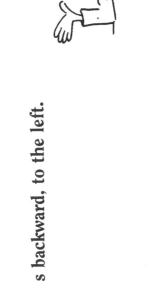

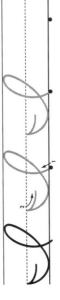

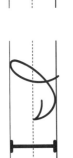

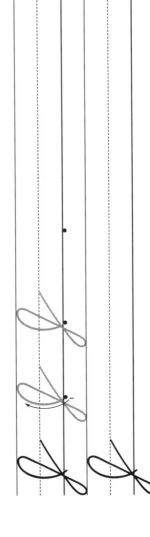

Try This!

Find out how many left-handed kids are in your class. Invite them to practice these letters on the board. Lefties only!

Name _____ Date _____

Curly Qs These letters have a fancy loop.

N n M m W w H h K k Z z

Trace and Write:

Cursive Writing With a Twist! Scholastic Professional Books

Capital Fun

We use capital letters in book titles. Make a real book cover and write the title in cursive. Use capitals for the first letter of each word.

Aa Bb Cc Dd Ee Ff Gg Hh Ii Jj Kk Ll Mm Nn Oo Pp Qq Rr Ss Tt Uu Vv Ww Xx Yy Zz

More Curly Qs

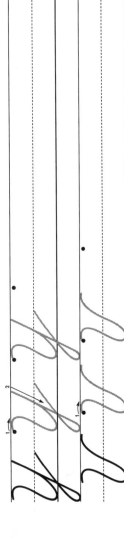

Uu Yy Vv Zz

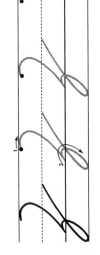

Nn Mm Ww Kk

Trace and Write:

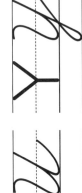

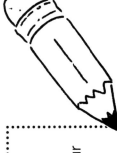

Capital Fun

We use capital letters in proper names. Write your name in cursive, capitalizing the first letter of both your first and last names. Practice all different ways of signing your name! Try the same with a friend's name.

Cursive Writing With a Twist! Scholastic Professional Books

Kickstarts

These start out with a little "kick"!

P P

R R

B B

Trace and Write:

Cursive Writing With a Twist!   Scholastic Professional Books

Aa Bb Cc Dd Ee Ff Gg Hh Ii Jj Kk Ll Mm Nn Oo Pp Qq Rr Ss Tt Uu Vv Ww Xx Yy Zz

Tabletops *T and F have their own fancy tabletops.*

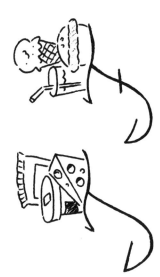

T

F

Trace and Write:

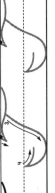

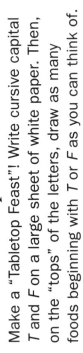

Cursive Writing With a Twist!   Scholastic Professional Books

Name _____ Date _____

Capital Mountains These are like mountain climbers, but bigger.

G g S s L l

Trace and Write:

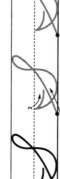

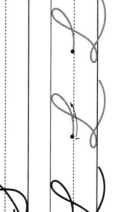
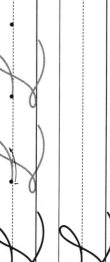

Capital Fun

Mr., Ms., Mrs., and *Dr.* are sometimes put in front of adults' names. Make a list of all the teachers you've had, including the prefix! Then, write and mail a letter to one of them, addressing the envelope in cursive.

Aa Bb Cc Dd Ee Ff Gg Hh Ii Jj Kk Ll Mm Nn Oo Pp Qq Rr Ss Tt Uu Vv Ww Xx Yy Zz

Write this tongue twister twice in cursive.
Say it twice, too!

Ann and Andy's anniversary is in April.

𝒜

𝒶

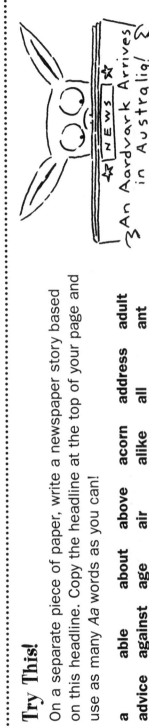

Try This!
On a separate piece of paper, write a newspaper story based on this headline. Copy the headline at the top of your page and use as many *Aa* words as you can!

a	able	about	above	acorn	address	adult
advice	against	age	air	alike	all	ant

Cursive Writing With a Twist! Scholastic Professional Books

Name _____

Date _____

Aa Bb Cc Dd Ee Ff Gg Hh Ii Jj Kk Ll Mm Nn Oo Pp Qq Rr Ss Tt Uu Vv Ww Xx Yy Zz

Write this tongue twister twice in cursive.
Say it twice, too!

Betty Botter bought some butter to make her batter better.

Try This!

On a separate piece of paper, copy and illustrate one of these tongue twisters and challenge a friend to read it:

Busy buzzing bumblebees.

The bluebird blinks.

Betty and Bob brought back blue balloons from the big bazaar.

Cursive Writing With a Twist! Scholastic Professional Books

Name _____   Date _____

Write this tongue twister twice in cursive.
Say it twice, too!

How many cookies could a good cook cook
if a good cook could cook cookies?

𝒞

𝒞

_____

_____

_____

_____

_____

Try This!

On a separate piece of paper, copy
this tongue twister and illustrate it!
Then challenge a friend to read it.

Clean clams crammed in clean cans.

Cursive Writing With a Twist!   Scholastic Professional Books

22

Name _____ Date _____

Write this tongue twister twice in cursive.
Say it twice, too!

Diddle diddle dee, diddle diddle dum.

Cursive Writing With a Twist! Scholastic Professional Books

Try This!
On a separate piece of paper, make up a story using some or all of these *Dd* words:

**daddy   daisy   dance   dandelion
dark   daydream   deep   dog**

23

Aa Bb Cc Dd Ee Ff Gg Hh Ii Jj Kk Ll Mm Nn Oo Pp Qq Rr Ss Tt Uu Vv Ww Xx Yy Zz

Write this tongue twister twice in cursive.
Say it twice, too!

$\mathcal{E}$

$\mathcal{l}$

Every elephant, especially Eleanor, needs extra eggs.

Name _____ Date _____

Write this tongue twister twice in cursive.
Say it twice, too!

Four furious friends fought for the phone.

Try This!
On a separate piece of paper, copy and illustrate one of these tongue twisters:

Friendly Frank flips fine flapjacks.

Fresh, french-fried fly fritters.

Five frantic frogs fled from fifty fierce fishes.

Cursive Writing With a Twist! Scholastic Professional Books

Aa Bb Cc Dd Ee Ff Gg Hh Ii Jj Kk Ll Mm Nn Oo Pp Qq Rr Ss Tt Uu Vv Ww Xx Yy Zz

Write this tongue twister twice in cursive.
Say it twice, too!

A gazillion gigantic grapes gushed gradually.

Try This!
On a separate piece of paper, copy and illustrate one of these tongue twisters:

Gobbling gorillas gobbled goblins.

George grabs a great green glob.

Name _____

Date _____

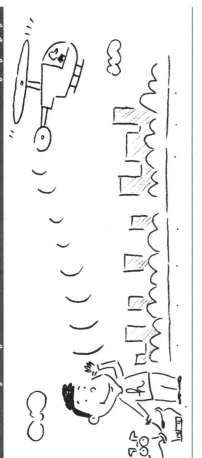

Write this tongue twister twice in cursive.
Say it twice, too!

Happy Harry hears a helicopter.

_____

_____

_____

_____

_____

_____

_____

_____

Try This!

On a separate piece of paper, write a newspaper story based on the following headline:

Huge Hurricane Hits, Helping Hands Help

Name _____

Date _____

Write this tongue twister twice in cursive.
Say it twice, too!

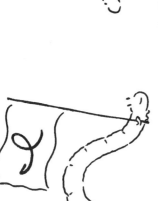

Inchworms inching, inch by inch.

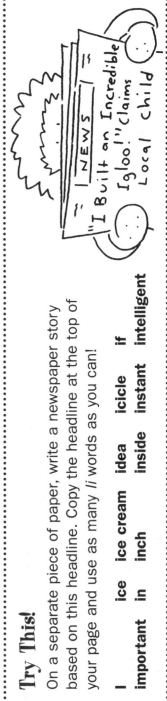

Try This!

On a separate piece of paper, write a newspaper story based on this headline. Copy the headline at the top of your page and use as many *Ii* words as you can!

I	ice	ice cream	idea	icicle	if
important	in	inch	inside	instant	intelligent

Cursive Writing With a Twist! Scholastic Professional Books

Aa Bb Cc Dd Ee Ff Gg Hh Ii Jj Kk Ll Mm Nn Oo Pp Qq Rr Ss Tt Uu Vv Ww Xx Yy Zz

Write this tongue twister twice in cursive.
Say it twice, too!

Jackie loves jumping jacks.

Try This!

On a separate piece of paper, write a news story for this headline. Copy the headline at the top of your page and use as many *Jj* words as you can!

joy	jellyfish	jam	June	jackpot
jungle	jolly	jiffy	job	jump

Cursive Writing With a Twist!   Scholastic Professional Books

Name _____

Date _____

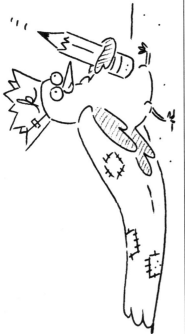

Write this tongue twister twice in cursive.
Say it twice, too!

Kooky Kookaburra thinks he's king!

K

K

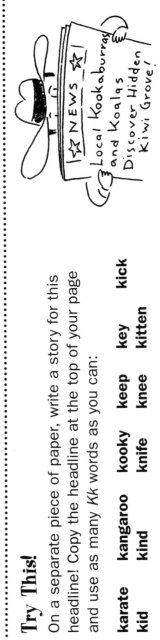

Try This!

On a separate piece of paper, write a story for this headline! Copy the headline at the top of your page and use as many *Kk* words as you can:

karate	kangaroo	kooky	keep	key	kick
kid	kind	knife	knee	kitten

Cursive Writing With a Twist! Scholastic Professional Books

Aa Bb Cc Dd Ee Ff Gg Hh Ii Jj Kk Ll Mm Nn Oo Pp Qq Rr Ss Tt Uu Vv Ww Xx Yy Zz

Write this tongue twister twice in cursive.
Say it twice, too!

Laura the ladybug licked luscious lollipops.

Try This!

On a separate piece of paper, write a story
using as many of these *Ll* words as you can!

lovely	lady	lemon	lollipop
lamb	ladybug	laugh	large
leap	learn	leave	little

Cursive Writing With a Twist! Scholastic Professional Books

Name _____   Date _____

Write this tongue twister twice in cursive.
Say it twice, too!

Mommy made me eat my M&M's.

_m_

_m_

Cursive Writing With a Twist! Scholastic Professional Books

Aa Bb Cc Dd Ee Ff Gg Hh Ii Jj Kk Ll Mm Nn Oo Pp Qq Rr Ss Tt Uu Vv Ww Xx Yy Zz

Write this tongue twister twice in cursive.
Say it twice, too!

Nate the newt never eats his noodles!

n

n

Try This!
On a separate piece of paper, copy
and illustrate this tongue twister:

A noisy noise annoys an oyster.

Cursive Writing With a Twist! Scholastic Professional Books

Name _____   Date _____

Write this tongue twister twice in cursive.
Say it twice, too!

Old oily Ollie oils old oily autos.

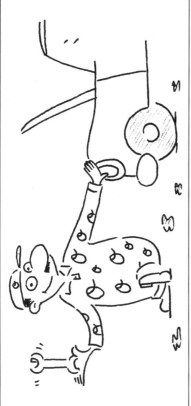

𝒪

𝒪

Try This!

On a separate piece of paper, write a newspaper story based on this headline. Copy the headline at the top of your page and use as many *Oo* words as you can!

oh	**occasion**	**off**	**odd**	**office**	**one**	**olive**	**omelet**
open	**opening**	**only**	**or**	**onion**	**out**	**other**

Name _____   Date _____

Write this tongue twister twice in cursive.
Say it twice, too!

Peter Piper picked a peck of pickled peppers.

P

P

Try This!

Pete the Pirate is peeved! Help him
tell people to stay off his property.
On a separate piece of paper, create
a sign that he can hang on his tree.
Remember to say "Please!"

Cursive Writing With a Twist!   Scholastic Professional Books

35

Name _____ Date _____

Write this tongue twister twice in cursive.
Say it twice, too!

Quick Kit, kick it quick!

Q

Q

Try This!
On a separate piece of paper, design and write
an advertisement for a new quilt store opened by
Aunt Quinn. Use as may *Qq* words as you can!

quilt	**quilting**	**quilted**	**quiet**	**quarter**
quick	**quickly**	**question**	**queen**	**quest**

Cursive Writing With a Twist! Scholastic Professional Books

Name _____

Date _____

Write this tongue twister twice in cursive. Say it twice, too!

Red rover, red rover, let Rory run over!

$\mathcal{R}$

$\mathcal{R}$

Try This!

On a separate piece of paper, design and make a menu for a new restaurant called *Really Rad Restaurant*. This restaurant serves only food that begins with *Rr*. Use these words or any other *Rr* words you can think of!

raisin	rhubarb
raspberry	ravioli
relish	roast beef
rock candy	rye bread

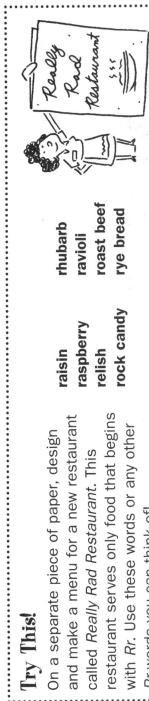

Name _____

Date _____

Write this tongue twister twice in cursive.
Say it twice, too!

Six sleek swans swim swiftly southward.

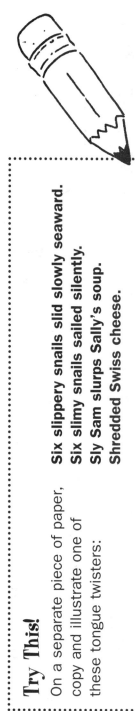

Try This!

On a separate piece of paper, copy and illustrate one of these tongue twisters:

Six slippery snails slid slowly seaward.

Six slimy snails sailed silently.

Sly Sam slurps Sally's soup.

Shredded Swiss cheese.

Name _____ Date _____

Write this tongue twister twice in cursive.
Say it twice, too!

Twelve twins twirled twigs.

Try This!

On a separate piece of paper, copy
and illustrate this tongue twister:

**The thirty-three thieves thought
that they thrilled the throne
throughout Thursday.**

Cursive Writing With a Twist! Scholastic Professional Books

Aa Bb Cc Dd Ee Ff Gg Hh Ii Jj Kk Ll Mm Nn Oo Pp Qq Rr Ss Tt Uu Vv Ww Xx Yy Zz

Write this tongue twister twice in cursive.
Say it twice, too!

Upside-down underwater urchins

𝒰

𝓊

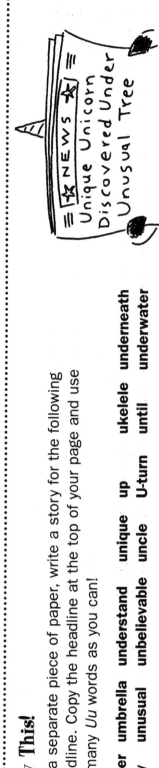

Try This!

On a separate piece of paper, write a story for the following headline. Copy the headline at the top of your page and use as many *Uu* words as you can!

under	**umbrella**	**understand**	**unique**	**up**	**ukelele**	**underneath**
ugly	**unusual**	**unbelievable**	**uncle**	**U-turn**	**until**	**underwater**

Cursive Writing With a Twist! Scholastic Professional Books

Name _____

Date _____

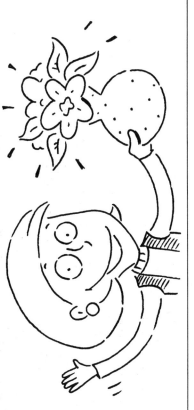

Write this tongue twister twice in cursive.
Say it twice, too!

Villagers visit with violets in vases.

Try This!

On a separate piece of paper, design a brochure for a fabulous adventure vacation! Use as many Vv words as you can:

very	vegetables	vacation	valley	volcano
vine	video games	vanilla	view	visit

Aa Bb Cc Dd Ee Ff Gg Hh Ii Jj Kk Ll Mm Nn Oo Pp Qq Rr Ss Tt Uu Vv Ww Xx Yy Zz

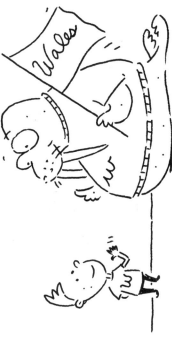

Write this tongue twister twice in cursive.
Say it twice, too!

Wayne went to Wales to watch walruses.

$\mathscr{W}$

$\mathscr{w}$

Name _____

Date _____

𝒳

Write this tongue twister twice in cursive.
Say it twice, too!

𝓍

Extremely excellent, extremely excellent!

Try This!

On a separate piece of paper, play "Exclusively X" tic-tac-toe with a friend! One player is lowercase *x*, the other is uppercase X.

Cursive Writing With a Twist! Scholastic Professional Books

Aa Bb Cc Dd Ee Ff Gg Hh Ii Jj Kk Ll Mm Nn Oo Pp Qq Rr Ss Tt Uu Vv Ww Xx Yy Zz

Write this tongue twister twice in cursive.
Say it twice, too!

Yippee yippee yip, yippee yippee yap!

Cursive Writing With a Twist!   Scholastic Professional Books

44

Name _____ Date _____

Write this tongue twister twice in cursive.
Say it twice, too!

Fuzzy Wuzzy wasn't fuzzy, was he?

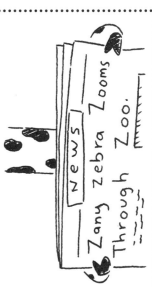

Try This!

On a separate piece of paper, write a newspaper story based on the following headline:

Zany Zebra Zooms Through Zoo.

Puzzles and Games

Aa Bb Cc Dd Ee Ff Gg Hh Ii Jj Kk Ll Mm Nn Oo Pp Qq Rr Ss Tt Uu Vv Ww Xx Yy Zz

First copy these sentences.
Then try to figure out what
makes them special!

Too bad—I hid a boot.

Don't nod.

Never odd or even.

Madam, I'm Adam.

A man, a plan, a canal—Panama.

Answer: They all read the same backward! This is called a palindrome.

Name _____ Date _____

Aa Bb Cc Dd Ee Ff Gg Hh Ii Jj Kk Ll Mm Nn Oo Pp Qq Rr Ss Tt Uu Vv Ww Xx Yy Zz

First copy these sentences.
Then try to figure out what
makes them special!

The quick brown fox jumps over the lazy dog.

Sixty zippers were quickly picked from the woven jute bag.

We promptly judged antique ivory buckles for the next prize.

Answer: Each uses every letter of the alphabet. This is called a pangram.

Aa Bb Cc Dd Ee Ff Gg Hh Ii Jj Kk Ll Mm Nn Oo Pp Qq Rr Ss Tt Uu Vv Ww Xx Yy Zz

Capital Letter Fun

**Say each letter out loud!
Then write out what they say
in cursive letters.**

I C D B

_____
- -
_____

M T

_____
- -
_____

I C U

_____
- -
_____

I V

_____
- -
_____

R U O K?

_____
- -
_____

Answers: I see the bee; empty; I see you; ivy; are you okay?

Name _____   Date _____

Aa Bb Cc Dd Ee Ff Gg Hh Ii Jj Kk Ll Mm Nn Oo Pp Qq Rr Ss Tt Uu Vv Ww Xx Yy Zz

Number Codes

Look at the numbers under each line.
Decode the secret message by matching
them up with the letters.

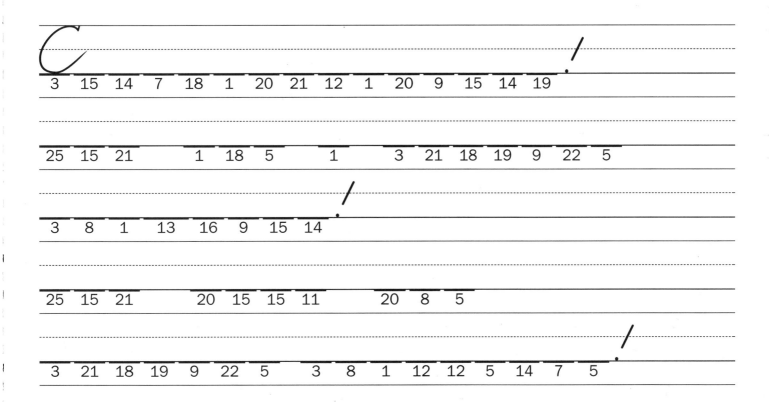

a	b	c	d	e	f	g	h	i	j	k	l	m
1	2	3	4	5	6	7	8	9	10	11	12	13

n	o	p	q	r	s	t	u	v	w	x	y	z
14	15	16	17	18	19	20	21	22	23	24	25	26

C _____ !

3 15 14 7 18 1 20 21 12 1 20 9 15 14 19

25 15 21   1 18 5   1   3 21 18 19 9 22 5

_____ !

3 8 1 13 16 9 15 14

25 15 21   20 15 15 11   20 8 5

_____ !

3 21 18 19 9 22 5   3 8 1 12 12 5 14 7 5

Now, on a separate sheet of paper, make up a number code.
Have a friend solve your secret message.

Answer: Congratulations! You're a cursive champion! You took the cursive challenge!

Cursive Writing With a Twist! Scholastic Professional Books

51

Cursive Consonant Collection

Write your own cursive alphabet list! Choose a category: animals, food, places, or names. Then write a word from that category that starts with each consonant. For instance: *bear, cat,* or *Bobby, Carl.*

Bb _____   *Nn* _____

Cc _____   *Pp* _____

Dd _____   *Qq* _____

Ff _____   *Rr* _____

Gg _____   *Ss* _____

Hh _____   *Tt* _____

Jj _____   *Vv* _____

Kk _____   *Ww* _____

Ll _____   *Xx* _____

Mm _____   *Zz* _____

Aa Bb Cc Dd Ee Ff Gg Hh Ii Jj Kk Ll Mm Nn Oo Pp Qq Rr Ss Tt Uu Vv Ww Xx Yy Zz

Sign Language

Have a friend spell a secret word letter by letter as you write it. Don't take your pencil off the page!

Name Poems

Write an acrostic poem for your name or a friend's name.
You can also use your last name and write a poem about
your family! Here's an example for the name "Liza":

Loves lemonade
Is good at spelling
Zoom! She's a fast runner
Amazing friend

Cursive Writing With a Twist! Scholastic Professional Books

Aa Bb Cc Dd Ee Ff Gg Hh Ii Jj Kk Ll Mm Nn Oo Pp Qq Rr Ss Tt Uu Vv Ww Xx Yy Zz

Scribble Script

Make a scribbly, squiggly design in the box. Don't take your pencil off the paper! Hide some cursive letters in your design, like this:

  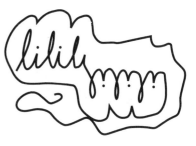

Then trade papers with a friend. Each person uses a highlighter pen to find the hidden cursive letters.

Name _____   Date _____

Aa Bb Cc Dd Ee Ff Gg Hh Ii Jj Kk Ll Mm Nn Oo Pp Qq Rr Ss Tt Uu Vv Ww Xx Yy Zz

Scrambler

Unscramble this grocery list. Write the words in cursive.

1. strocar
2. tubert
3. cleare
4. roful
5. slapep
6. grusa
7. ainrsis
8. ancob
9. cluette
10. etithpags

1.
2.
3.
4.
5.
6.
7.
8.
9.
10.

Cursive Writing With a Twist! Scholastic Professional Books

Aa Bb Cc Dd Ee Ff Gg Hh Ii Jj Kk Ll Mm Nn Oo Pp Qq Rr Ss Tt Uu Vv Ww Xx Yy Zz

Scrambler

Unscramble this egg recipe! Use the letters below each blank to complete the recipe in cursive.

An Eggstra-Special Treat

From the kitchen of _____
(Write your name here.)

4 _____   _____
    lisces   **derab**

6 _____
    gges

1½ cups _____
           kilm

¼ _____   _____
  upc   **rhecdda**   **eechse**

¼ _____   _____
  upc   **wsiss**   **eechse**

¼ _____   _____
    ponoseat   **stal**

½ _____ *frozen hash brown* _____
  upc   **seottaop**

Arrange _____ _____ *across a*
      derab   **lisces**

greased baking pan. Beat together all remaining

ingredients and pour over _____. *Refrigerate*
                      derab

overnight. Bake at 350 degrees for 40 to 45 minutes.

Aa Bb Cc Dd Ee Ff Gg Hh Ii Jj Kk Ll Mm Nn Oo Pp Qq Rr Ss Tt Uu Vv Ww Xx Yy Zz

Capital Letter Scramblers

There's something special about these arrangements of cursive capitals. What is it?
Read these words up, down, and across! Write all the words you find in lowercase cursive.

G E L
E Y E
L E G

_____

R A T S
A B U T
T U B A
S T A R

_____

T R A P
R A J A
A J A R
P A R T

_____

Aa Bb Cc Dd Ee Ff Gg Hh Ii Jj Kk Ll Mm Nn Oo Pp Qq Rr Ss Tt Uu Vv Ww Xx Yy Zz

Cursive Word Search

**Highlight all the words you find in this word search!
Remember all the cursive terms you learned.**

agckickstartipenciln
gamountainclimber
quoscriptsmoothness
dpenoblumpylettersi
exbackwardballoons
postureytabletopsw
sleftiesacursivelsize
uspacingycurlyquo
fidownhilldaredevil
tishapezgpppaperidm

My style of writing sure is new—
Here's a note from me to you!

Aa Bb Cc Dd Ee Ff Gg Hh Ii Jj Kk Ll Mm

Nn Oo Pp Qq Rr Ss Tt Uu Vv Ww Xx Yy Zz

The Cursive
A B C Book

1

Aa Bb Cc

2

Dd Ee Ff

3

Gg Hh Ii

4

Jj Kk Ll

5

Mm Nn

6

Oo Pp Qq

7

Rr Ss Tt

8

Uu Vv Ww

9

Xx Yy Zz

10

Write your full name in cursive.

Cursive Writing With a Twist! Scholastic Professional Books

Name _____ Date _____

Uppercase and Lowercase Letters

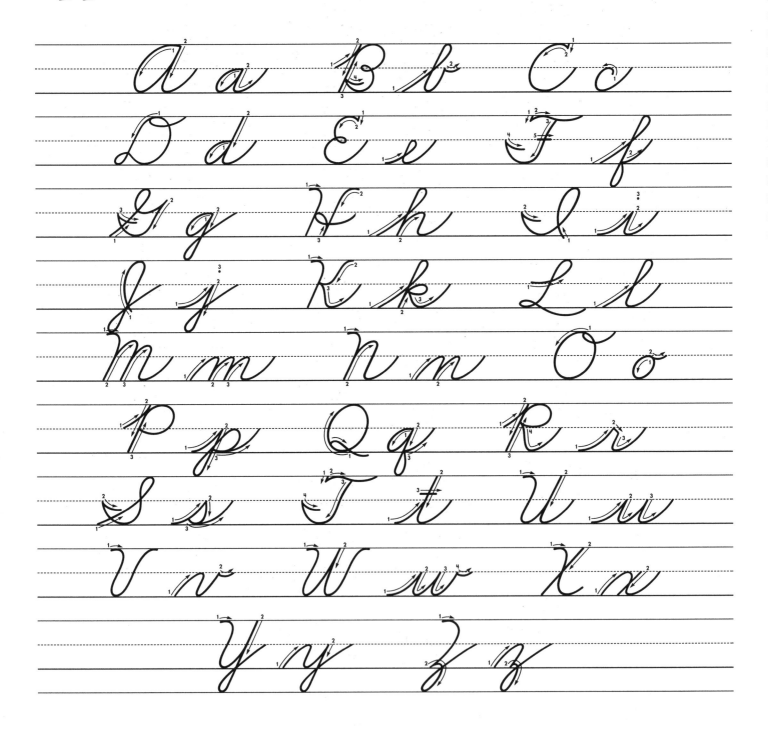

Cursive Writing With a Twist! Scholastic Professional Books